How Rabbit
Lost his Tail
and other stories

Adapted by Sheila Lane and Marion Kemp

Illustrations by Joy FitzSimmons

Take Part Starters

Level 1

Ward Lock Educational Co. Ltd.

Ward Lock Educational Co. Ltd.
1, Christopher Road
East Grinstead
Sussex
RH19 3BT

A member of the Ling Kee Group
London • New York • Hong Kong • Singapore

© Sheila Lane and Marion Kemp
This edition published 1991
ISBN 0 7062 5154 7

Printed in Hong Kong

Contents

★ This sign means that
you can make the
sounds which go with
the story

How Rabbit Lost his Tail

This is Rabbit, who has a fine, bushy tail when the story begins.

This is Fox, who plays a trick on Rabbit.

Rabbit is walking along the road by the river.

Rabbit I do believe I can see old Fox coming
this way. Hallo Fox!

Fox Hallo, Rabbit!

Rabbit Have you been for a nice walk by the river?

Fox Not me!

Rabbit You look mighty pleased with yourself.
Don't tell me you've got a nice fat fish
for your supper in that bag. I don't believe it!

5

Fox Look in my bag.
One. . .two. . .three. . .four. . .five!

Rabbit One. . .two. . .three. . .four. . .five! Five fat fish.
I don't believe you caught those fish.

Fox Oh, yes I did.

Rabbit You must be a mighty fine fisherman to catch
five fat fish. I don't believe you caught them
yourself. I think you're fooling me.

Fox I'm not fooling you.

Rabbit I just fancy a fine, fat fish for my supper.

Fox If you want a fish, you go and catch one.

Rabbit How can I catch a fish when I haven't got a hook and line?

Fox You can catch a fish with your tail.

Rabbit What! How can I use my fine, bushy tail to catch a fish? Stop fooling me, Fox.

Fox I'm not fooling you.

Rabbit All right! You show me how to catch a fish with my tail. We're just on the river bank. Tell me what I have to do.

Fox Just sit on the bank and dip your tail
in the water.

Rabbit All right. Ow! The water's cold! Ow! Ow!

Fox Just sit on the bank and keep still.

Rabbit Ow! Ow! Ow! The water is freezing. How will
I know when there is a fish on my tail?

Fox Just sit on the bank and keep still.

Rabbit I shall freeze to death if I stay here much
longer. Do you think I've caught a fish yet?

Fox Not yet.
Just sit on the bank and keep still.

Rabbit I don't believe this is the way to catch a fish.
Are you fooling me, Fox?

Fox No, I'm not fooling you.

Rabbit But my tail is freezing.
Is it time to see if I've caught a fish yet?

Fox No, not yet.

Rabbit But the water has frozen all round my tail.

Fox Just sit on the bank and keep still.

Rabbit Fox! Fox! Did you hear something plopping in the water?

Fox No.

Rabbit Listen! I can hear PLOP! PLOP! PLOP! ★

Fox Is it a fish?

10

Rabbit How do I know? I can't move. My tail is stuck in the ice. Help! Get me out!

Fox How can I get you out?

Rabbit Pull me out! Go on! Pull me out! Go on, Fox. Pull harder! You're not trying.

Fox Oh yes I am.

Rabbit Pull harder. Count to three, then PULL.

Fox One . . . two . . . three . . . PULL!

Rabbit Oooooooo! My tail's gone! Oooooooo!
Ooooooo! My fine, bushy tail has snapped off
in the ice.

Fox You haven't got a tail now, Rabbit.
The fish have got your tail now.
Ha, ha! Ha, ha!
You haven't got a tail!

*And from that day to this all rabbits have had short
tails.*

Things for you to do

1

This is a fat fish.

Draw five kinds of fish and colour them in.

2 A rabbit's home is *under the ground.*
Write: *Things which live under the ground* on your paper.
Draw things which live under the ground.

3 Write these sentences in the right order for the story.

Next he dipped his tail into the water.
First Rabbit sat on the bank.
Soon the water froze round his tail.

4 How many animals can you think of with long tails?

Draw the pictures and write the names of the animals.

The Miller, his Son and their Donkey

This is the Miller.   This is his son.

The Miller and his son are walking along the road.
They are taking their donkey to sell at the market.

14

Son   Come along! Come along!
Trot on, donkey, or we shall never get
to market. ★
Is it far now, father?

Miller No, it is not far now.

Son   Trot on, donkey. Trot on. ★
I'm getting tired.
Listen!

Miller What is it?

Son Look at those girls over there.
They are laughing at us. ★

Miller What if they are?

Son They are calling us fools.

Miller What if they are?

Son Well, perhaps we ARE fools. We have a
donkey to ride and yet we are both walking.

Miller Get up, then.
Get up on the donkey.

Son Ah! This is better than walking.
Trot on, donkey, then we shall soon get
to market. ★
Is it far now, father?

Miller No, it is not far now.

Son Trot on, donkey. Trot on. ★
Listen!

Miller What is it?

Son Look at those men over there.
       They are calling me a lazybones. ★

Miller What if they are?

Son Well, perhaps I AM a lazybones.
       The men are saying that it would do me good
       to walk.

Miller Get down, then.
       Get down off the donkey and I will get up.

Son Very well.
Trot on, donkey, then we shall soon get
to market. ★ Is it far now, father?

Miller No, it is not far now.

Son Trot on, donkey. Trot on. ★
Listen!

Miller What is it?

19

Son Look at those women and children over there.
They are calling you a lazy old man. ★

Miller What if they are?

Son Well, perhaps you ARE a lazy old man.
The women and children are saying
that you are riding in comfort,
while I have to follow on my own two legs.

20

Miller Get up, then.
Get up on the donkey with me.

Son Very well. That's better!
Now we're both up on the donkey.
Trot on, donkey, then we shall soon get
to market. ★
Is it far now, father?

Miller No, it is not far now.

Son Trot on, donkey. Trot on. ★
Listen!

Miller What is it?

Son   Look at those people over there. They are saying that we are unkind to our donkey. ★

Miller   What if they are?

Son   Well, perhaps it IS true. The donkey is very tired. I know! We had better carry him.

Miller   No! No! We can't do that.
We can't carry the donkey.

Son   Oh, yes we can. Look! Here is a strong pole. We will tie the donkey's legs together and then we can give HIM a ride.

Miller I don't like this at all.

Son Come on, father. Lift when I say THREE.
One. . .two. . .THREE. LIFT!
Good! Now let's trot on.

Miller I can't trot on.
I'm not a donkey.

Son We are nearly there. I can see the market.
Once we have crossed the bridge over the
river we shall be there.
Listen!

Miller What is it?

Son Everyone is laughing at us. ★

Miller What if they are?

Son But we are ON the bridge. The donkey can hear everyone making a noise. He's kicking! Keep still, you silly animal. Keep still! Hold him, father! Hold him!

Miller I can't hold him.

Son He will be in the water if we can't hold him.

Miller I . . . CAN'T . . . HOLD . . . HIM!

Son Oh! Oh! He's going over the edge!
Going! Going! ★

Son GONE!

Miller And now we have no donkey.

Son What fools we both are!

So the Miller and his Son pleased nobody AND lost their Donkey.

Things for you to do

1

This is the donkey.

A donkey is an animal.
Draw five other animals
and colour them in.

2 The donkey was being taken to be sold at the market.
Write: *At the Market.*
Draw some more animals which could be sold at a
market.

3 Write these sentences in the right order for the story.

Then they both rode on the donkey.
First the son got up on the donkey.
Next the miller got up on the donkey.

4 How many things can you think of that you would like
to buy at a market?

Draw the pictures and write the names.

Anansi and Snake

This is Anansi
the Spider Man.

This is Snake.

One day the Animals said to Anansi: 'If you can catch Snake, we will promise to call all our stories, The Anansi Stories.' So Anansi sat by Snake's hole and waited.

28

Snake Good morning, Anansi.

Anansi Good morning, Snake.

Snake Why are you sitting by my hole, Anansi?
Are you trying to catch me?

Anansi No, no, Snake.

Snake I think you ARE trying to catch me, Anansi.

Anansi No, no, Snake.

Snake Oh, yes you are. You think you CAN catch
me, don't you?

Anansi No, no, Snake.
I don't think I can catch you.

Snake Then why don't you go home
to your little leaf house?
Why do you just sit and look at me like that?

Anansi I like to sit and look at you, Snake.

Snake Well, I *am* good to look at. Did you know
that I am the longest animal in the world,
Anansi?

Anansi No, I didn't know that.

Snake   I'm longer than that bamboo tree over there.

Anansi   I didn't know that.
You cannot be longer than
that bamboo tree.

Snake   Of course I am!
Look! I will come right out of my hole
and show you.
Now! Am I very, very long?

Hole Sweet Hole

Anansi Yes. You are very, very long.

Snake Am I longer than the bamboo tree?

Anansi The bamboo tree is very, very long, too, Snake.

Snake Look here, Anansi. I am much longer than that bamboo tree.
You go and cut it down and I'll show you.
Do as I say. Cut it down.

Anansi I will. ★
I will cut it down now.

Snake Cut all the branches off.
Do as I say. Cut the branches off.

Anansi I am. ★
I am cutting the branches off.

Snake Now put it down on the ground beside me
and I will lie on it. There!

Anansi You are not on it, Snake.

Snake What do you mean? Of course I am on it.
Look! My tail is right at the end.
Go and see.

Anansi Your tail is at this end, Snake . . .
BUT . . .

Snake Now come up to the other end.
Look! My head is at the other end.

Anansi Yes, BUT . . .

Snake What do you mean, BUT . . . ?

Anansi Your head is at this end . . .
BUT . . .
When your head is at this end,
your tail is not at the other end.

Snake Ho! Ho! So you think I am crawling up
and down the bamboo tree, do you Anansi?

Anansi No, no. I did not say that.

Snake You miserable little Spider Man.
You think I'm cheating, don't you?

Anansi No, I don't.

Snake I'll show you that I'm not cheating.
Tie my tail to one end of the tree.
Go on. Do it.

Anansi I will.
I will do it now.

Snake So! My tail is tied to one end of the
bamboo tree.
Now watch me stretch my head up to the
other end.
Go on. Watch me S-T-R-E-T-C-H!

Anansi Go on, Snake. S-T-R-E-T-C-H!

Snake Am I nearly there, Anansi?

Anansi No, no! Not yet.

Snake Then I will stretch again.
Am I nearly there this time, Anansi?

Anansi Go on, Snake. S-T-R-E-T-C-H!
SHUT YOUR EYES and S-T-R-E-T-C-H!

Snake All right. I'll shut my eyes
and make one big effort.
Now . . . one . . . two . . . three . . .
S-T-R-E-T-C-H!

Anansi GOT YOU!

Snake Ow! Ow! Stop it, Anansi.
You're hurting my neck.
Untie the string from round my neck.
I can't move.

Anansi I've got you, Snake,
and I'm going to keep you!

And from that day to this all the animal stories were called: The Anansi Stories

Things for you to do

1

This is a snake.

Draw the snake and colour
in the patterns on its body.
Draw and colour some
more snakes.

2 A snake is *long.*
Write: *Things which are long.*
Draw things which are long.

3 Write these sentences in the right order for
the story.

Next he cut off the branches.
Then Snake said that he would lie on it.
First Anansi cut down a bamboo tree.

4 String is used for tying things.
What else can be used for tying things?

Draw the pictures and write the names.